Ideas for Kick Butt Businesses

Table of Contents

<u>*Introduction*</u>

"Now Is the Time to Start Your Own Home Business!"

Hello! In case you don't know me, my name is James Jones and I publish a weekly newsletter called, "Kick Butt Business Ideas" as well several information products about starting your own home based business.

Over the past several months I have been searching for the very best home business ideas to share with my readers. Included in this ebook are 12 of those businesses. Businesses that I believe anyone with a little bit of drive and spunk can start tomorrow and be profiting from very quickly.

If you are looking to start your own home based business get ready for an "Ah-Ha" experience!

Whether you are a stay at home mom, stressed out corporate executive, cash poor student or fixed income senior, whatever your current situation, you will find the ideas presented in this ebook to be a breath of fresh air.   No Get-Rich-Quick-Schemes here. Just solid business plans that will work if you apply yourself and expend just a little effort.

Looking to start a part-time business just to bring in a few extra bucks each month? No problem! Most of these businesses can be started on a part-time basis so you can work when you want.

Here are my "cream-of-the-crop" business ideas. Let get started!

"The Lazy Man's Way to Create and Sell Highly Sought-After Niche Info Products on the Internet!"

Do you remember the final scene from the movie, "Indiana Jones and the Raiders of the Lost Ark?"

In case you haven't seen it or don't remember, Indiana Jones goes in search of the _Lost Ark of the Covenant_ which is the chest in which the original 10 Commandments are housed.

The year is 1939 and the Nazis – who want to use the Ark as a weapon -- have uncovered the town which is supposedly the Arks final resting place.

Jones is hired by the American government to find the Ark before the Nazi. And to make a long story short, he does.

At the end of the movie we see Jones meeting with an unnamed Army Intelligence Official to discuss the fate of the Ark. He is assured that the Ark will be studied and that they have "the best men working on it now."

Indiana Jones is not satisfied with that answer but there is nothing he can do about it.

In the epilogue the viewer sees what really happens to the Ark: It's crated up and stored in a warehouse along with thousands of other non-descript crates housing other forgotten artifacts awaiting study.

Of course, none will ever be studied. They are simply stored away –
presumably to keep them out of the hands of the bad guys.

So what does Indiana Jones and the Raiders of the Lost Ark have to
do with you making money with *Niche Info Products*?

Only this...

I have discovered a virtual warehouse full of forgotten treasures
worth potentially billions of dollars!

This warehouse contains the collective group of creative works that
have quietly disappeared into the Public Domain.

If you're not familiar with the term "public domain" allow me to give
you a general idea of the legal and business power contained in
these two words. At a very basic level, "public domain" means...

**...anything that is NOT protected under US copyright law.
This includes ALL works published before 1923 AND, under
certain conditions, works published up to 1978. A 'work' can
be anything: a book, a play, music, photographs, movies,
manuals, reports, posters, etc...**

Re-publishing and re-packaging public domain information and other
creative works can make you a lot of money. The reason is fairly
simple:

If you find, re-package and sell information that has fallen into the
public domain you do not have to pay royalties or copyright fees on
that work. Can you tell me about any other business that you can
resell over and over and keep 100% of the profits without paying
ONE CENT in royalties or copyright fees for its use?

In any normal business start-up you will be required to provide a Tax
ID number along with other documents and a proof of your business
registration just to be able to buy your products for resale! Then,

until you've had a chance to establish 'terms' with your wholesaler, you'll be required to pay cash, up front, for your entire starting inventory.

If you're buying widgets for $4.95 wholesale and selling them for $9.95 you must constantly re-invest that $4.95 in more widgets. In order to do a large trade in widgets you'll need a large inventory! Before you even open your business door you'll have to invest $50,000 to $100,000 in widgets and as soon as you sell one of them you have to take $4.95 out of that $9.95 sale and plunge that right back into buying more widgets! I call it the 'black hole' of retail business, because you will constantly have up to $100,000 or more, depending on the type of business you operate, tied up in cold, hard inventory for as long as you are in business!

Let's contrast this normal business start-up with one that is started using 100% FREE public domain information as their 'widget'.

First, I should state clearly that there is not another business in the world that is more profitable than the 'information business' i.e. selling books, manuals, reports, etc...

But...

The biggest problem for most individuals who want to enter this enormously profitable business is that they have to either create their own information product or secure the rights to sell someone else's product. For most individuals 'creating' their own information product is very hard to do... they can't write or don't like to write, they find it difficult or impossible to even think about writing an entire book!

If you love the idea of publishing information as a business model but you don't want to create your own book or manual...what do you do?

Sell Public Domain Information!

First, securing the rights to public domain information will cost you nothing- they are 100% free to use!

Second, there are thousands of works to choose from in thousands of categories. And since almost no one knows this opportunity exists you will be able to dominate entire markets before your competition even knows what hit them!

Third, since you do not have to purchase a large stockpile of inventory and you have no major competition you can spend your money where it matters most: creating marketing that makes you money!

There are books and manuals and music and other creative works whose copyrights expire almost every day. These are all potential information products that are FREE for the taking, if you know how to find them and how to re-publish them!

In fact, the vast treasure of public domain information is growing daily and a very tiny, miniscule percentage of the business public even know that they can be used without permission, without cost and without royalties or fees.

Using Public Domain words is absolutely the easiest way to start or expand an existing business with low risk and high profits! Your product is 'free' and when you sell it you keep 100% of the profits. If you ever see a better opportunity, please let me know!

This is a massive opportunity that has been created because thousands of books, music, movies and other 'works' have passed into the public domain in just the last few months and years.

Public Domain works are the perfect products to sell on the internet!

Since they cost you nothing to acquire your only cost is in duplication. Or, you can digitize the work and sell a downloadable version that costs you nothing.

Want to see an example? I thought you would never ask! ☺

Here is a product I created from a public domain book I found in my local library. The book was called "Arts and Crafts for Home Decoration" and was written in the 1920's. It's basically a handicraft manual with chapters on making dolls, lamp shades, embroidered envelope pocketbooks, crocheted handbag, and many other items.

So I took the chapter on making dolls, scanned it and reprinted it into a little booklet that I re-titled, "Illustrated Doll Making Instructions."

I then listed the booklet on eBay. Here is a partial image of the auction:

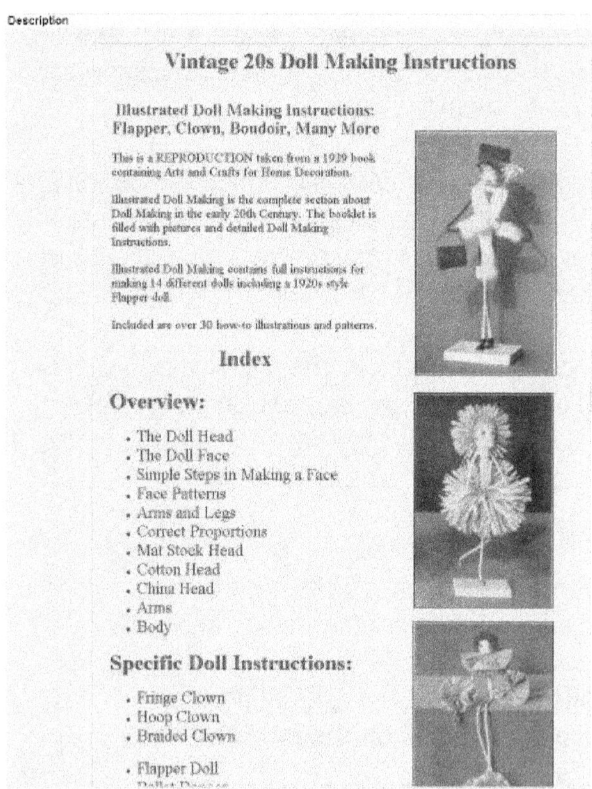

That particular auction sold for $14.00. Not a lot of money, to be sure. But, my product cost was only what it cost me to have it copied – about 75 cents -- at my local self service print shop.

But, here is the important part: I now OWN the rights to this new booklet that I created from the original book. And since it is <u>my own product</u> I can make as many copies as I want and sell as many copies as I can – for a cost of only 75 cents per copy. (if I had it mass printed I could probably get the per copy price down to 25 cents or less)

But, it gets better…

From that one auction I had 8 unique bidders. So, after the auction ended I sent the seven losing bidders a "Second Chance Offer."

> Note: Second Chance Offers are a little used – but very powerful -- feature offered by eBay. Basically, a Second Chance Offer can be sent to any of the non-winning bidders if the winning bidder does not pay the seller, if a seller has duplicate items, or the reserve price is not met in a Reserve Price Auction. Second Chance Offers can be created immediately after a listing ends for up to 60 days. Second Chance Offers contain a *Buy It Now* price equal to the non-winning bidder's bid amount.

Out of the seven Second Chance Offers I sent three bidders took me up on the deal for an average *Buy It Now* price of $10.00. That turned into an additional $30.00 profit that took me about 1 minute to achieve. I have continued to re-list that same booklet several times and it has sold each time – at a final price of between $7.00 and $22.00.

That is just one small example of republishing Public Domain products. If I had the time I would locate other Public Domain books on *doll making* and create a website on the subject. I am sure the market exists for this type of information since I had no problem selling several copies of the first booklet.

I have another product that I have been experimenting with in the Art Category. It's a reproduction of a print taken from an 1890's book on Mushrooms.   The print was yellowed and old looking so I took it to Kinko's and they were able to digitize it, clean it up and electronically remove the yellowing. They charged me $10.00 for the cleaning plus $1.00 per print (it's a large poster sized image)
Here is a (reduced) picture of the print:

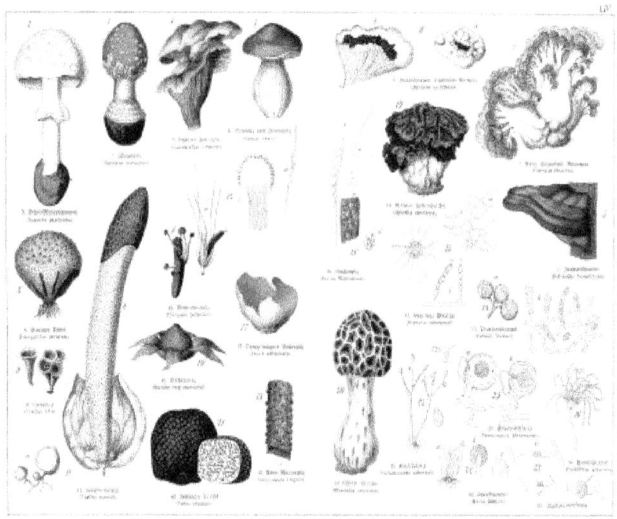

Pretty cool, huh!

There are thousands of works in the public domain- they are simply 'there' - you don't have to do anything to create them- they are just there waiting to be re-published and they are ALL FREE!

You can do exactly what I did... reprint the information, create an 'ebook', create posters, framed 'prints, your own line of coffee cups, mouse pads, etc... and sell them on eBay.

As I mentioned, when you find a work that's in the public domain you can digitize it (with a scanner hooked up to your computer) you can have it published as a 'real book' and sell it on Amazon, or sell it as an ebook or even create a 'course' and publish it!! The possibilities are endless and the profits staggering.

Not every kind of work in the public domain will have a market but here are some examples of books you could be re-publishing that have an excellent market right now:

Books on mind reading, thought transference, etc
Books on marketing, advertising and copywriting
Books on trading stocks and commodities
Books on collecting: figurines, Wedgwood, pottery, etc
Books on hand writing analysis, palmistry and the occult
Books on herb remedies and natural healing
Children's books and stories
Posters (the 'patriotic' ones are especially popular right now)
Radio shows, music and movies!

How Can You Tell If a Work Is In The Public Domain?

Here's a general guide to what is and what is not protected under copyright   (Note: This Applies Only to Printed Works Published in the US):

1. If the work was published in the United States prior to 1923, it is in the public domain.

2. If the work was published in the United States between 1923 and 1978 without a copyright notice, it is in the public domain.

3. If the work was published in the United States between 1923 and 1963 with a copyright notice, but copyright was not renewed 28 years after the first registration, it is in the public domain.

4. Any work published after 1978 should be considered NOT in the Public Domain EVEN IF it does NOT have a copyright notice.

5. Most (but not all) US government works are automatically in the Public Domain.

Ok, I know it's confusing. Between 1923 and 1963 the "test" of whether a work is in the Public Domain is if the copyright was renewed after expiration or not.

So, what is the safest route to getting started with republishing Public Domain works?

Only republish printed works that were first published in the US before 1923. Those works are definitely in the Public Domain.

About 93% of the books published in the US between 1923 and 1958 are also in the Public Domain (because the copyright was not renewed after expiration) BUT it is important to do a copyright search in order to be certain.

Where to find Public Domain Works

The best place to start is your local library. Simply browse the shelves in the subject areas that interest you and look for books published in the US before 1923. You can then check them out, copy them – in whole or part – republish, and resell them.

You can also find Public Domain works online by searching the inventory of online book dealers at http://www.abe.com and http://www.alibris.com/.

With thousands of books, manuals, reports and other works available, republishing Public Domain information offers entrepreneurs with one of the best money making opportunities of this decade.

**Are You Ready To Open this Treasure Chest of Highly Profitable Public Domain Works? Detailed information on profiting, finding and re-publishing public domain information is available from:
www.PublicDomainTreasureChest.com**

"Adventures of a Spyware Detective"

You have probably heard the saying that you can make money by "finding a need and filling it." Well, here is a huge need in the form of a problem that hundreds of thousands of computers users have. And they don't know how to solve this problem themselves even though the solution is fairly simple.

The problem is Spyware (also known as scumware or adware).

Spyware is a term for hidden software programs that reside on the user's computers and do things such as transmits user information via the Internet to advertisers or display pop-up ads.

In many cases these programs slow down the user's computer and make it difficult and frustrating for the user to complete simple computing tasks. Users usually get these programs when they download free software such as games or use a file or music sharing utility.

You can offer a low cost *Spyware Removal Service* to computer users in your area.

For a fee of, say, $25.00 you go to their location and remove all the spyware from their computers.

Removing the spyware is a simple task with the help of some free spyware and adware removal utilities. There are several of these utilities available but the two I recommend are:

Ad-Aware – available from:
http://www.lavasoftusa.com

Spybot – available from:
http://www.safer-networking.org

You can download both these applications for free and put them on a CD which you can then install on your client's computers.

You can also offer a service where you install a firewall on your client's computers for an additional charge.

A firewall is a must-have for any computer that is connected to the internet with a high speed connection (such as broadband or cable modem) to keep hackers from getting access to the computer.

The firewall I recommend is:

Zone Alarm – available from:
www.zonelabs.com/store/content/home.jsp

To get business run an ad in the classified that reads...

Computer Running Slow? I will come to your location and remove Popups, Spyware and Adware from your computer. $25 Service Call. Call 555-555-5555

If you are feeling particularly adventurous you can also phone businesses in your area and offer a free "diagnosis service" where you come out and check their computers for problems. Once you find the problem you can then offer to fix it for a fee.

You can also sell other services such as physically cleaning their computers, installing hardware, upgrading memory, etc.

The time to start this business is NOW! This problem exists with just about every computer and now you know how to solve it.

**Excerpted from Emergency Cash Generators. For 101 Quick and Easy Money Making Ideas see:
www.EmergencyCashGenerators.com**

"Fast Cash with Club VIP Cards"

The concept for this technique came about while I was in the restaurant business about 12 years ago.

I was the manager of a small "mom and pop's" type restaurant doing pretty well until a competitor moved in next door and started really cutting into our business. We decided to fight back with a promotion aimed at local businesses.

Now, if you have ever done any advertising -- in the newspaper, direct mail, Penny Savers -- or other traditional methods, you know the response rate is very low compared to the circulation. A direct mailing that pulls 2 people out of 100 is considered outstanding.

Newspapers and other printed media usually pull way less than 1%. I remember placing a 2 for 1 coupon in the local newspaper that only pulled in 2 customers out of 200,000 circulation!

Not wanting to repeat our past failures we decided to try something a little different. We printed up business cards with our logo and the text. The card looked something like this:

Mom and Pop's Restaurant
Courtesy of your employer: Buy 1
Meal get the second Meal Free

8508 Carowinds Blvd   803-555-1212

Free meal must be of equal or less value. Offer expires
06/30/1990. By Law State Tax is calculated on total value of
both meals.

Then we drove around to all the office parks within about a 3 mile radius of the restaurant and passed the cards out to all the businesses and offices.

What we would do is walk up to the receptionist, introduce ourselves as managers of the restaurant and tell her we would like to give 2 for 1 VIP cards to all the employees.

We must have passed out cards to 200 offices and not a single one turned us down. Many of them included the discount cards in their employee's pay envelopes. The rest either passed them out or put them in each individual employee mail box. We achieved almost 100% distribution.

We passed out the first batch of cards on a weekday afternoon -- right after lunch. The next day I was scheduled to be in at 12:00. At 11:30 my phone rang. It was the general manager calling to see if I could come in ASAP because they were slammed. Truthfully, it didn't even cross my mind it was the cards bringing in the extra business. I just assumed it was a full tour bus which we would sometimes get during summer.

I arrived at about 11:50 and noticed there were no buses parked in the parking lot -- but the line of customers was out the door!

As I walked in and saw people -- local business people -- waiting to be seated I remembered the cards. All these people were there to use their discount cards.

We were slam busy up until about 2:30. Finally, we got everybody fed and then scrambled to adjust the schedule to handle the added volume for the next few days. Then we went out and passed out more discount cards.

Our lunch business continued to be brisk for the next week. After the dust had cleared and we counted the cards that had been redeemed, we were absolutely shocked to find 22% of the cards had been used!

That is an amazing redemption rate by any standards. The cost was just what it costs us to have the cards printed less distribution.

Why was the response so good? I have a few ideas:

1. The phrase "Courtesy of your employer" makes it sound like the employer arranged for the employees to receive the discounts cards. This makes them more valuable than if you just passed them out yourself.

2. The receptionists "talked it up" to the employees because they recognized what a good deal it was.

3. We were actually getting out there and meeting people face to face which is good PR.

How does this translate into you making money?

Easy -- create a VIP discount card you pass out to local businesses -- and they in turn give to their employees. You want to make it look like this card is a perk or benefit the business offers their employees.

Here is a sample of one such card:

S. Charlotte VIP Card -- $10.00

This Special VIP Card is sponsored by your employer. Use it to at participating retailers to save 15% or more on your purchases. Expires 07/31/2002. See attached sheet for specifics and participating businesses.

Notice the $10.00 price. This price is just a "suggested price." You don't actually charge for the cards. It's worth $10.00. But the employee doesn't have to know their employer didn't pay $10.00 for it! The suggested price is on the card to increase perceived value. If the employee thinks the card costs $10.00, she is more likely to use it.

Now what you do is get out your local newspaper, shoppers, penny savers and anything else with print ads. Call the businesses that have advertised in these papers and tell them you are distributing 5,000 VIP cards to the employees of local businesses and you would like to include their offer on your card. The cost is $25.00 for 5,000 cards distributed to local employees. The cards will expire in 1 month.

The offers for each individual business can be included on a separate piece of paper that is 1/3rd of an 8 1/2 x 11 sheet which you can staple to the cards. You could get 100 or more offers on each 1/3rd page sheet.

The best way to work this is to spend a day calling the businesses and selling spots on your VIP card sheet. If you can sell 10 the first day you have earned $250.00. Get their ad copy over the phone. Just ask them if they would like to run the same offer that was in the newspaper. Tell them you will be out the next day to collect the money. The next day, go out and collect the money and spend the rest of the day on the phone selling more.

At $25.00 each, if you only got 25 ads, you would gross $625.00. Your costs would be about .03 cents each for the business card and attached sheet. That works out to $150.00 for 5000 so your profits would be $475.00. You can easily distribute 5000 VIP cards in a day by going to businesses in business parks and to factories with a lot of employees.

This is a super simple but extremely profitable business anyone with a little drive and spunk can do tomorrow.

"How to Start a Fun, Rewarding and Profitable Special Event Letters to Children Business in Your Area (and become a Community Hero to boot)"

It should come as no surprise that children love to receive mail. Even in this age of instant communication via email, cell phones and text messaging the thrill a child gets from receiving an honest-to-goodness personal letter *addressed to them* in the mail is hard to beat.

Now, you can provide children in your area with that same excitement, anticipation and the absolute thrill of discovering a personalized letter addressed *to* them and written *about* them in their mailbox.

In this report I am going to give you the details of a specific plan of action for starting a *Special Event Letters to Children* Business in Your Area. As a side benefit of this plan you will also be helping non-profit organizations in your community raise desperately needed funds.

Very simple, what you will be doing is working with a non-profit organization to hold a fund raising event where you will sell a Special Holiday Letter to Children. Proceeds collected will be given to the non-profit organization. After the event you can then follow up with the parents and offer them your complete *Special Event Letters to Children* package for an additional fee.

There are several holidays that lend themselves to fund raising events including: Christmas (*Letter from Santa*), Easter (*Letter from the Easter Bunny*), Valentines Day (*Letter from Cupid*), Halloween (*Letter from the Great Pumpkin*) and Independence Day (*Letter from Uncle Sam.*) You can organize fund raising events throughout the year and maintain a steady flow of fresh customers.

Let me give you an outline of the plan and then I will go into the specific steps in more detail:

1) Locate a Non-Profit Organization you would like to work with to raise funds.
2) Pitch your event to the non-profit organization.
3) Find a suitable high traffic Location to set up Your Fund Raising Event.
4) Get everything ready to set up your event.
5) Notify the local media about your event.
6) Hold the event.
7) Follow through and follow up.

Locate a Non-Profit Organization you would like to work with to raise funds.

Helping a non-profit organization gives you the benefit of tying your product to their organization. It gives you instant credibility in the eyes of the donors (customers) and also gives you an inroad when dealing with media outlets and merchants who will allow you to use their location for the fundraiser. The best type of organization to work with is a locally based children's charity. It is much easier to deal with a local charity then it is to deal with a local branch of a national charity and local charities are always in desperate need of cash.

You should be able to find a local children's charity in your Yellow Pages. Check under the headings: Social Service Organizations, Human Services Organizations and Charitable Organizations. If you can't locate one call your local United Way office. They can point you in the right direction.

Pitch your event to the non-profit organization.

Selling the charity on your fund raising event should be the easiest
part of your task. You can offer to do all the work yourself and they
would only need to lend their name to the event. Or, they may be
willing (or even insist) that they have one or two of their volunteers
on hand to make sure everything runs smoothly and that the
interests of the charity are being protected.

You need to listen to their needs and be as flexible as possible. It is
absolutely crucial to your success that the charity is happy. Above all
be honest and up-front about what you are doing. Let them know
both what <u>they</u> will get out of the event and what <u>you</u> will get out of
it (i.e.: prospects for your *Special Event Letters to Children* business.)
One successful event will lead to many more in the future.

You will need to set a price for the Holiday Letters and let the charity
know how much they will receive. I suggest a price of $5.00 per
letter because this is a small amount that most people will have on
hand as they are shopping.

Note: It is critical to realize that with this Fund Raising Event you are
NOT trying to make money from the Holiday Letters. You will make
your money from the sale of the *Special Event Letters* package.
Structure this event so it crystal clear to everyone – the charity,
merchants and customers – that all profit will be going to the charity.

The absolute best option is to give the charity 100% of the *proceeds.*
However, this will mean that you will have to go out-of-pocket to pay
for postage and material costs of sending the letters. The next best
option is to offer the charity 100% of the *profits.* This way you can
take out the cost of sending the letters. Whatever you do make it
absolutely clear up front how much the charity will make per letter.
If you are working this from the 100% profit angle this means you
will need to know how much it costs you to create and mail each
letter. Since you will also be sending a separate follow-up letter to
the parents advertising the *Special Event Letters* package you will
want to consider the cost of this follow-up letter as well. At the very

most I would not recommend allocating more than $1.00 per letter for expenses. This gives the charity a very attractive 80% of the proceeds and allows you to recoup your expenses.

Find a suitable high traffic Location to set up your Fund Raising Event.

The task of finding a high traffic location is made much easier by the fact that you have associated yourself with a worthwhile charity. Approach a merchant with the idea of selling Letters from Santa from his store and you will no doubt be turned away 9 out of 10 times. But, add that you are raising money for "Make a Wish" or "Special Olympics" and you immediately gain their willingness to help out.

Which merchants should you approach? You want a location with lots of walk through traffic. Inside a mall would be ideal. Or, right outside a busy grocery store. Or, even a children's restaurant – such as Chucky Cheese.

You'll need to call up the manager of the mall, grocery store, etc and tell them what you would like to do. It also would not hurt to tell them that you will be mentioning their store in the press release that you will be sending to the media. Free publicity is always a good thing.

Your event needs to be held on a weekend. Saturday is best but you might also try to get permission to run the event for the entire weekend. If your event is to be held outside you need to figure out what to do in case of rain. Can you set up inside instead? Can you reschedule for a different weekend?

After you get a firm date send a letter to the manager and your charity contact confirming the time, date and other details. You want to make absolutely sure that everyone is clear about when the event will be held.

Get everything ready to set up your event.

You will need to get several things ready for your event. You will need a Table (such as a folding card table) and chairs for people manning the event. From the front of the table you need a big sign that advertises the event.   For example, if you are doing an Easter fund raiser the sign would read:

Personalized Letter from the Easter Bunny for Your Child!   100% of Profits Go To (Charity Name). Only $5.00

It is best if you have the sign professionally made -- like the vinyl signs you see hanging from the outside of restaurants and retail stores. You may be able to get the sign donated by a sign shop. If not – and you don't want to spend the money to get the sign made – you can make one yourself with white poster board and a black marker. Make sure the sign is legible from several yards away.

You'll also need to have several hundred order forms available and plenty of pens. Once again, you may be able to get this donated. (check with an office supply store for photocopying and pens)

Have a copy of a sample letter filled out to show your prospects. Indicate on the sample in bold print where the personalization will be. For example the sample would have the name of the child, their street, age, etc. all in bold print. You could even have the letter enlarged to poster size and position it so it stands up on the table for easy viewing.

Another thing you can do that will really get people's attention is to give away something to the children who pass by. A bookmark, stickers or some other small, inexpensive giveaway would be great.

It would also add to the atmosphere if the people working the booth dressed up as holiday characters. At the very least you can holiday specific hats from a costume shop or party supply store.

Notify the local media about your event.

The media will almost always publicize worthy charity events. In order to notify the media you can use a Press Release.

A Press Release is a page or small packet of information that is mailed or faxed to the media to encourage them to give some attention to a particular event.

You will find a sample press release at the end of this section that you can modify for your event.

The press release should be on the non-profit organizations letterhead if possible. If they do not have a letterhead, type a basic one using MS Word or any good word processing software. The letterhead should include the name of the organization, address, and phone number. This information should be at the very top of the page.

On the next line include the date of the Press Release. Date your press release the day you expect it to be received. This is done so that an editor or reporter does not confuse your press release with an older press release or older material.

The press release should also include your name, phone number and address at the top of the page where it can be seen easily by an editor or reporter.

Address the release to the editor in charge. Make a phone call to the newspaper or station and ask who the appropriate person would be and address your press release accordingly.

Send the press release to local newspapers, regional magazines, radio stations, television stations, and weekly newspapers.   Send it out at least 10 days before the event and then again three days before the event.

On the next page is a sample press release that you can modify for your event:

555 Main Street
PO Box 555
Charlotte, NC 55555

Make a Wish Foundation

Press Release

Date: 10/20/2004

Contact: Jane Doe, Coordinator

Phone: (555) 555-5555 E-Mail: janedoe@aol.com

Subject: Letters from the Easter Bunny Fund Raising Event

For Immediate Release

(City, State): A *Letters from the Easter Bunny* fund raising event for Make a Wish Foundation will be held at the Carmel Crossing Shopping Center at 8508 Carmel Rd on Saturday, December 4th from 9:00 A.M. until 3:00 P.M. Funds will be raised for operational expenses of the Make a Wish Foundation Volunteer Center.

100% of the profits from the sale of *Letter from the Easter Bunny* will be donated to the Make a Wish Foundation Volunteer Center.

Parents can purchase a personalized *Letter from the Easter Bunny* that will be mailed to their child right before Easter. Parents fill out a short questionnaire which will be used to personalize their child's letter. The fee for a personalized *Letter from the Easter Bunny* is only $5.00.

This event is being sponsored by *Fun Mail for Kids* and the Carmel Crossing Harris Teeter. Free stickers will be handed out so be sure and bring your children.

###

Hold the event.

On the day of the event you will need to get all your materials together and set up at your prearranged location. Be sure to give yourself enough time to get set up before the event – at least 30 minutes. It's also a good idea to check in with the manager to let them know that you have arrived.

I recommend you have at least two people manning the table. One should roam around and pass out the treats to the children and encourage the parents to look at the sample letter. The other should stay close to the table and answer questions, take money, make change, pass out the order forms, etc.

Note: when I say "treats" I mean some type of low cost handout such as bookmarks or stickers. Do not hand out candy.

Follow through and follow up.

After the event you will need to distribute the money to the charity minus the agreed upon percentage for your expenses. Then immediately get to work sending out the letters.

A couple of weeks after you send the letter send a follow up letter to the parents promoting your *Holiday and Special Event Package* of letters.

I suggest you create two packages of letters. One package of 6 holiday letters plus one special event letter.

Note: Special event letters are letters for the child's Birthday, Tooth Fairy (sent when a baby tooth is lost), Summer Checkup from Santa.

For this package I would charge $25.00. The second package would have 10 holiday letters and two special event letters for $39.00.

For either package the parent would choose which letters they want to be sent from a selection form that you will provide when they order.

Note: The Tooth Fairy letter will need to be sent when the child loses a tooth. So, I suggest you include a postcard that the parent will mail back to you at the appropriate time to let you know to mail the letter.

Here is a breakdown of what to send and when:

Approximately two weeks after you send the Fund Raising Holiday Letter send a letter to the parents advising them of your *Holiday and Special Event packages.* Include information about the different packages you offer, pricing, a sample personalized holiday letter, a selection form -- to indicate which package they want and which letters -- and a return envelope.

When they send payment you should immediately send a personalization form that they will fill out to tell you the child's custom information.

It is very important to send this form only <u>after</u> you have received payment. The reason for this is because if you include the personalization form with the initial product information many people who would like to order will procrastinate about filling out the form and they will end up not ordering.

After you receive the personalization form you should make a copy and send back to them for their records. Also include a few postcards that they can mail to you in case any of the information changes (for example, if their pet goldfish dies you would not want to refer to the goldfish in a letter) as well as a post card for the Tooth Fairy letter if needed. Include instructions telling them when to use the postcards and confirm when the letters will be mailed to their child.

Keep a calendar of when to send the letters and mail them as scheduled.

We have created a special "Holiday and Special Event Package" that includes 25 special event and holiday letter templates. You can customize these letters with each child's specific details. Included in this package of letters are:

Tooth Fairy
Birthday
Easter
Flag Day
Independence Day
Halloween
New Years
St Patrick's Day
Thanksgiving
Valentines
Mothers Day
Pre-Christmas
Christmas Check Up

Each letter uses a special character to give the child interesting and fun facts about the specific holiday or to encourage the child to develop good habits such as brushing their teeth.

Multiple letters are included for most occasions in the cases where there are more then one child receiving the letters in the same household. This way, you can send a different letter to two or more children in the same household for the same Holiday.

The "*Holiday and Special Event Package*" is included free when you purchase "*Letters from Santa.*" For details visit: www.KidsMailFun.com

"How to Profit From Highly Targeted Local Email Newsletters"

This concept is simple:

Pick a topic that generates a lot of interest in your area then create a free emailed newsletter that focuses on that topic. Make money by selling advertising in the newsletter to individuals and businesses.

One topic you might consider is the Restaurant Sanitation Inspection Reports.

Don't laugh -- when presented in a tabloid journalist style these things can be really interesting and controversial. People have both a morbid curiosity and a genuine interest in knowing what kind of things were found in the food at their favorite restaurants.

Restaurant Sanitation Inspection Reports are public record and should be freely available in your area.

Another topic you might focus on is Yard Sales. Currently the only place people having yard sales can advertise in is the newspaper or in "take one" shoppers. Create a free weekly emailed newsletter that lists all the area yard sales and provides more information than a small classified ad in the newspaper.

At first you'll have to get your listings from the newspapers but as you grow you can begin charging people to list with you.

Here is one that I think has a lot of potential: *Lunch Special Email*

Contact (by telephone) 5 NICE but casual restaurants and tell the manager that you have a newsletter that features the lunch specials of different restaurants in town and that the readers have chosen his restaurant as one of the best in the area. (hey you are not fibbing about this... just don't tell them that your newsletter only has one reader -- you! And your list of restaurants constitutes your first issue.)

Now, tell the manager that you are running a promotion with the first prize being lunch for 2 for a week at the best restaurants in the area. Ask him if he would donate a Gift Certificate redeemable for lunch for 2 people. Tell him he will get free advertising for a week in return.

Keep doing this until you have 5 gift certificates from 5 different restaurants.

Next, go to retail or service type stores in your area and tell them that you are running a contest giving away lunch for a week at 5 different restaurants. Tell them if they will allow you to place a fishbowl (to collect signups) on their counter that you will give them free advertising in your newsletter. Look for places like dry cleaners, Mail Box Etc., coffee shops, hair dressers, tanning centers, nail salons (concentrate on businesses that have a lot of walk in traffic and cater to women)

Try to get 5 or 6 in the same general area. Have non-competing stores (only one in each category)

You will need to have some entry forms printed up. Any printer can do this for you or you can do it yourself on your computer. You will need the following information:

    Name
    Work Email address
    Zip Code

Leave a fish bowl, a sign with details of the contest, a pen (attached to a string that is attached to the fishbowl) and the entry forms on the counters of the stores that agree to your offer.

You may have to haggle to get the store managers to agree. Stress that you will be emailing 2000 people and you will include his offer for free. Be sure to tell him that you will only accept one store from each category so he will not have any competition.

You can also take entry forms to office parks and hand them out to the receptionists in the different offices. Ask if they will pass them out to the workers there. You can collect them later.

Once you have 2000 names, pick a winner and send them an email letting them know they won. Send everybody that didn't win an emailing telling them that although they didn't win first prize they did win second prize which is one year's subscription to the *Lunch Bunch Letter* which contains lunch specials and discounts from area restaurants and other businesses.

At first, publish the restaurants specials for free. You want the newsletter to have 10 -- 15 restaurants included. Then approach each restaurant and ask if they would pay $25.00 a week for the service. Get a 3 month commitment (along with a check!) Stress exclusivity! ("We only want to feature one Italian restaurant and since YOU are the best I thought I would offer you first shot at it before I take it over to Caruso's...")

Publish one newsletter with 10 -- 15 restaurants for every 2000 subscribers. So if you have 4000 subscribers publish 2 newsletters with 2000 subscribers each, etc, etc, etc.

Excerpted from Secret Underground Business Ideas. For More Unusual but Profitable Money Making Ideas see: www.UndergroundBusinessIdeas.com

"The Ultimate Work at Home Opportunity: Start Your Own Virtual Assistance Business"

One of the hottest business endeavors today is virtual assistance. Starting your own virtual assistant business is relatively inexpensive, and armed with the proper information and determination, you can excel in this growing field.

Why start a virtual assistance business? Simple: With the ever-changing face of business in the 21st century, there is only one thing that remains certain: businesses — particularly small businesses and independent professionals — are always in need of high-quality assistance ranging from data entry and transcription to legal advice and tax counsel. Many times small businesses simply can't afford to hire employees to take care of the nitty-gritty details for which they don't have time, and oftentimes small businesses need help, just not full-time help.

Also, if you've ever worked in business, you're aware that businesses are always in search of ways to cut costs and save money. Virtual assistants do just that. We'll look at how virtual assistants help save businesses money in a few minutes, but first let's answer the question: what exactly is a virtual assistant?

Quite simply, a virtual assistant is an individual who provides services for businesses or professionals over the Internet. Communication is generally done online—although there may be phone conversations as well. Files are sent back and forth via email or fax, and completed work is returned the same way.

Virtual assistants may have clients in their hometown and they may have clients across the country or halfway around the world. There is no limit to where a virtual assistant can work or what services she can offer. Virtual assistants often never even meet their clients face-to-face.

Finally, virtual assistants generally do not work for only one business or one professional, instead working for numerous clients, whether long-term or on a one-time basis.

As a virtual assistant, you can offer a plethora of services. Think about your strong points. Are you an accomplished secretary? Is desktop publishing your forte? Do you have a law background that would allow you to offer legal assistance? The possibilities for the services you can offer really are endless.

You can offer as many or as few services as you'd like. Just make sure you are strong in the services you are going to offer. It's obviously better to offer one service in which you excel rather than a handful of services in which your expertise is only marginal.

Let's take a list of the services a Virtual Assistant can offer. Remember this is only a partial list, and you may think of many more services you can offer.

- Accounting
- Bookkeeping
- Data entry
- Desktop Publishing
- Dictation
- Event Planning
- Internet Research
- Legal
- Mailing
- Marketing

- Phone support
- Proofreading
- Secretarial
- Transcription (medical, legal, etc.)
- Translation
- Travel Arrangements
- Web site design and maintenance
- Word Processing

How much can you expect to earn?

How much you earn depends in large part on how much you will charge. Some virtual assistants charge as little as $10 per hour while others charge as high as $50 per hour. However, the current average rate ranges from $25-$35 an hour. There are several factors you'll want to consider when setting your rates.

First, do some market research. For example, if your virtual assistant business is going to be offering data entry, research what other virtual assistants in your area are charging clients per hour for data entry. You can find other virtual assistant businesses by doing an online search, using the phone book or checking with your local Chamber of Commerce.

You also want to assess your level of experience. If you're a beginner then you certainly won't want to charge as much as if you have ten years of solid experience behind you. As you gain more and more experience, you'll be able to raise your rates.

Once you determine the average going rate and factor in your experience level, you'll want to set your own rates. The key is to find a so-called happy medium. You don't want to set your rates too high, or you'll price yourself out of the market. On the other hand, you don't want to set your rates too low, otherwise you'll likely raise some eyebrows. If you charge too low, potential clients are going to wonder why? Are you inexperienced? Are you unreliable? Why are your rates so low? Remember the old saying, "You get what you pay for." Your potential clients will likely be thinking that as well.

If you're offering specialized services, such as legal or web design, you'll likely charge much higher per hour rates.

Instead of charging a per hour rate, you may want to charge on a per project basis. If you choose to do so, you'll want to consider several factors including an estimated number of hours the project will take, expenses (long distance phone calls, travel, etc.) and scope of the project.

Why is the market hot for virtual assistants?

As we noted before, businesses are always on the lookout for ways to save money, and virtual assistants do just that. By contracting your services, businesses benefit in a variety of ways including:

- You already have your own equipment.

- You are an independent contractor, which means businesses are not responsible for paying your social security and Medicare taxes, health insurance, unemployment, worker's compensation or vacation and sick pay.

- You will work for them only when they need you, thus saving them the cost of a full or part-time employee.

- You work from home or from your own office, thus the business doesn't have to find space for you.

- By developing a relationship with you, businesses don't need to hire temporary employees. Temporary employees often have to be brought up to speed quickly, and they usually do not have the opportunity to develop a relationship with the business as you will.

- As a virtual assistant, you can offer flexibility to businesses both in the hours you work and the way you are paid. (As a virtual assistant and independent contractor, you can be paid either by the hour or by the project, whichever you decide is best for you.)

Virtual assistants are also usually highly-qualified individuals who need little instruction and guidance. An employer gives you a project, and you run with it, checking in only when you have questions and to give periodic updates.

All of the benefits we discussed can play a role in your marketing campaign, for these are the reasons businesses should use your services.

How much will it cost to start your business?

Starting a virtual assistant business is relatively inexpensive, especially considering you probably already have most of the equipment you'll need: a computer, an Internet connection, a phone with an answering machine and a fax.

Most computers already come equipped with some sort of fax program, and you can usually find a printer/scanner/copier combination for around $100, a worthy investment.

Do you already have an office in your home? If not, is there an area you can designate specifically for your virtual assistant business? This is important for tax purposes; ask your tax consultation for specific details.

Aside from the equipment you'll need, you also need to take into consideration the legal issues. Will you need a business license to operate a business from your home? Check with your local government and state government to determine their rules and regulations.

Once you've decided on a business name, you'll need to determine whether or not it must be registered. If your name last name is Thomas, for example, and you call your business Thomas' Virtual Assistance, you won't need to register your name simply because you're using your name.

However, if you name your business Excellent Virtual Assistants, you will need to register your name. To determine how to register your name, including fees involved, go to http://www.sba.gov/world/states.html and click on your state.

Market, Market, Market

With the mere mention of the word marketing, some people begin to panic, thinking a successful marketing campaign means shelling out a lot of money. The good news is that's just not true. You can market your virtual assistant business with a little bit of money and a lot of creativity. The key to success is persistence.

First and foremost, you need to identify your market. Are you going to focus on small businesses? Big businesses? Individual professionals such as graphic designers, writers and accountants?

Deciding who your market is will help you tailor your written material, such as postcards, to your specific audience.

Establish a web presence. Your first marketing task, above all else, is to establish a web presence. There is no question that a web site is essential for individuals and businesses competing in today's business world. Your website is your virtual business card, and it will give you the opportunity to show off your skills, your services and what you can do for your potential customers.

The first choice you have to make is whether you're going to hire someone to design your website or you're going to do it yourself. Hiring a design pro can cost you anywhere from a few hundred dollars to several thousand dollars. Remember, though, that the key to marketing is creativity. So, you might consider contacting your local community college or college and ask if there is anyone in the graphic design department who would like to design your website. You can offer a fee and give your permission, so the designer can use your website in his or her portfolio. Students are generally eager to gain experience and samples to put in their portfolios.

If you would like to design your own website but have little experience, you can generally do so with little difficulty. Many community colleges offer adult education classes that generally run anywhere from four to six weeks with classes meeting for a few hours each week. You should have no trouble finding an inexpensive adult education course that will teach you HTML and how to design your own website in a relatively short period.

If you don't have the time and want to get your business started quickly, then it's time to take to a trip to the library or to your local bookstore. There are plenty of books that will guide you through the process. Following are a few books you might want to flip through when deciding what book will be your guide:

- Creating Web Pages for Dummies, Sixth Edition, by Bud Smith and Arthur Bedlan.

- Learning Web Design: A Beginner's Guide to HTML, Graphics, and Beyond by Jennifer Niederst.

- Professional Website Design from Start to Finish by Anne-Marie Concepcion.

- Web Design: A Beginner's Guide by Wendy Williard.

- Web Design Complete Reference by Thomas A. Powell.

Finally, there is a third way to establish a website quickly and effectively. There are numerous websites online that offer novices free web templates. You can browse through the many templates offered, download the one you like best and make the design changes you want while adding your own content. It is important to note that some template designers require you give them credit for the design of the site while others allow you to use the template without any credit given.

Following are several websites that offer free templates for your use. You can find more by putting "free templates" in Google, Yahoo or another search engine:

http://freesitetemplates.com/ -- Offers free as well as inexpensive templates.

http://www.freewebtemplates.com/ -- Choose from hundreds of free templates or browse through the many links to other free template sites.

http://www.interspire.com/templates/ -- Offers dozens of free templates, site frequently updated and a free newsletter.

http://www.fuzzywebmaster.com/ -- Find dozens of free templates in addition to articles on Internet marketing and resources for webmasters.

http://www.free-templates-layouts.com/ -- In addition to free templates and layout, you'll find links to several dozen other free template websites.

Business cards. Another effective, inexpensive marketing method is using your business cards. Always make sure you carry your business cards with you. Another excellent piece of advice, from marketing experts, is to hand potential clients and new contacts two business cards. This way the person can pass your business card along to someone else who might be interested in your services.

When you design a business card, make sure you make the most of the space you have. Think about the typical business card: you generally only find writing on one side, right? That's a lot of wasted space on the flip side, space you can effectively use.

On the front of your business card, you'll want to include all of the pertinent information including your name, phone number (both office and cell, if viable), email address or addresses and the URL to your website. Maximize the room on your business card by using the back to list the services you offer or any other information you would like to share with the client.

Offer discounts. Bring new clients to your virtual assistant business by offering an introductory discount. Some new small businesses offer substantial introductory discounts of 40 percent or more while others decide to stay on the more conservative side. Either way, offering a discount can be a key factor in getting a potential client to "take a chance" on you.

Join a virtual assistant forum or listserv. Just go to Yahoo Groups, and you'll find a plethora of forums and listservs to join. This is a great way to share your knowledge of the business with fellow virtual assistants. You'll also find the opportunity for networking is high. One word of caution, however, before you begin posting. Make sure you don't use the forum or the listserv as a platform to sell your services. This is highly frowned upon and could get you banned from posting.

Write letters to the editor. Read the newspaper, paying close attention for any articles that relate to your expertise or your virtual assistant business. Then, write a clear, concise letter to the editor asserting your opinion in a professional manner. When you sign your name, make sure to add your business name and URL. The Opinions section is one of the most read sections of newspapers. So, there is a good chance someone who needs your services might read your letter and decide to check out your website, potentially leading to new business.

Start spreading the word. Have you ever noticed when someone is really unhappy with a product or a service, he tends to tell everyone about it? Happy clients can do just the same for you—if you ask them. If you have satisfied clients then ask them if they wouldn't mind telling their friends, coworkers and others about your services. You might even ask them if they mind giving your business card to anyone they think might be interested in your services.

Word-of-mouth is one of the easiest and cheapest ways of building your client base. It is also one of the most effective. After all, you have someone who has used your services and who is satisfied. There is nothing more effective than the recommendation of a satisfied customer.

Join your local business organization. Every town and city has business organizations. You're probably most familiar with your local Chamber of Commerce. Joining the Chamber of Commerce in your community is an excellent way to network. Chamber of Commerce chapters generally list their members, along with their contact information and URL, in a publication that is published yearly, and there are monthly events in which members get together.

Write free articles. There are thousands of ezines on the Internet today, and many of them are desperate for quality articles. Let's say, for example, one of the services you offer is medical transcription. You might want to write an article about how to get into medical transcription: from securing the right education to finding a job. Find an ezine into which your article will fit and submit it. Always make sure when submitting an article you are allowed to put a brief biography at the end of the article that includes your website URL.

Writing free articles is an excellent way to establish yourself as an expert in your field as well as a way to get more people to come to your website. There are also article "libraries" to which you can submit your articles. Anyone looking for an article on your topic may then use it as long as they include your biography and website URL.

Send postcards. Sending postcards is an expense, but it's not a big expense. The big advantage of postcards is once you have your client base established mailing postcards on a monthly basis allows you to keep your business in the forefront of your clients' minds. It's also an excellent way to offer discounts or to invite your clients to look at your website.

If you do decide to go the postcard route, you can create your own postcards inexpensively by purchasing postcard paper at your local office supply store, designing them with your publishing software then printing them yourself.

Joining Professional Organizations

A great way to network with other virtual assistants and to become involved in the virtual assistant community is to join a virtual assistant professional organization.

Many times these organizations offer education just for members, listing of your business in their member directory and support.

Links to Virtual Assistant Organizations

- International Virtual Assistants Association. The IVAA offers its members a wide range of benefits, including listing in the member directory. It is also the only virtual assistant organization that offers its members Virtual Assistant Certification. The site is open to non-members as well as members.

- International Association of Virtual Assistants. The IAOVA provides members with information on web hosting, reselling of web hosting (another way to make a profit), FrontPage Templates, scholarship information, articles, a worldwide directory and a host of other benefits.

- Virtual Business Group. The Virtual Business Group is a worldwide organization dedicated to helping virtual assistants and includes marketing advice, opportunities to apply for grants, a links page and a membership directory.

Links to Helpful Small Business Organizations

- <u>Small Business Administration</u>. The Small Business Administration is the place to go to get small business advice, free of charge, from business advisors as well as the first stop to learn everything you need to know—from implementing your business idea to helping your business expand once it is running. They also have a free business card listing of which you'll definitely want to take advantage.

- <u>SCORE: Counselors to America's Small Business</u>. SCORE is an invaluable asset to America's small business owners. In addition to offering valuable business seminars at minimal cost, SCORE has knowledgeable business counselors who will meet with you for free to assist you.

- <u>National Association for the Self-Employed</u>. As a business owner, you are self-employed, and the NASE is an excellent resource for support, information and many benefits for members. Annual membership is currently $134.

- <u>The American Small Businesses Association</u>. Members of the ASBA are eligible to apply for grants, offers health insurance and valuable support.

If you are looking for a business where you can spend most of your time working from home, starting your own virtual assistant business can be the key to achieving your financial and personal dreams.

"How To Make Your Fortune as a Modern Day Wheeler-Dealer"

In the old days a wheeler-dealer had a reputation as being a shrewd person who knew how to circumvent difficulties in order to achieve a certain result. Typically the wheeler-dealer had knowledge or know-how that others didn't possess and they used this knowledge as leverage in order to realize a profit.

Wheeler-dealers of the past were often considered to be unscrupulous con men.   But, that is an unfair assessment to the true wheeler-dealer of today who helps to facilitate win/win situations and creates profits where none existed before.

Take the case of a friend of mine...

Last month she facilitated 1349 such "deals" which generated an average profit of $65.98 each. In return for her knowledge and know-how she took 40% of the profits and gave her partners 60%.

This 60% represented a return for the partners that they would not have been able to achieve themselves so they were happy to allow my friend to keep 40% of the profits.

If you run the numbers you will see that my friend grossed just a bit over $89,000.00 in one month. She took $35,602.80 as her 40% cut. That represents a typical month for her eBay Auction Consignment business.

What exactly is an eBay Auction Consignment business?

An eBay Auction Consignment is a process where one person – a consignee – agrees to sell items for another person – a consignor -- on the eBay auction site.

The two people enter into a written agreement whereby the consignee will sell the consignor's items for a certain fee or percentage of the final sale price.

The consignee is responsible for...

- Writing a detailed description of the items.
- Photographing the items.
- Listing the items on eBay.
- Handling questions from bidders.
- Collecting payment from the buyer.
- Packing and shipping the item.
- Customer service.
- Paying the consignor.

Why an eBay Auction Consignment business is the perfect work from home venture.

Many people have heard of eBay but they are unsure how to go about listing their items. To the inexperienced potential eBay seller the process can seem very intimidating and complicated. Many people who could benefit the most by listing their items on eBay – such as Pawn Shop Brokers, Specialty Store Owners, Artisans, Crafters, Antique Shop Owners – may have thought about using eBay as a selling tool but gave up the idea because they didn't have the time or knowledge to figure it all out.

That is where you come in. By starting an eBay Auction Consignment Business you can help these retail and specialty store owners move their unwanted or overstocked items and make an extraordinary income for yourself.

Here are a few of the many advantages that an eBay Auction Consignment Business offers you…

- Allows you to start your business immediately without investing money in expensive inventory.
- Has low start up costs -- generally all that is needed is a computer, internet connection and a few basic office supplies.
- Requires no employees.
- Can be operated on a part-time basis.
- Has low on going (variable) expenses.
- Enables you to work with a variety of different retailers so you always have new and exciting items to sell.
- Has very high income potential -- profits of $20,000 or more per month are not unusual.

To start an eBay Auction Consignment Business you will need the following:

Knowledge of the eBay Auction process. If you are not already familiar with selling on eBay I suggest you go through eBay's Free Training Course and begin selling unwanted items you have around your house. This will allow you to develop your selling skills and develop your feedback rating.

When you are ready to begin selling for others you should put together a Presentation Package consisting of the following:

- A description of your Consignment Services
- A List of Benefits to the Consignor
- A print out of several successful sample auctions
- A print out of your feedback rating
- List of your fees
- Consignment Contract

Take your Presentation Package to local businesses: Pawn Shops, Artisans, Antique Dealers, etc. Tell them you can generate extra cash for them by selling their excess and slow selling inventory on eBay.

Schedule an appointment to meet with them to go over their excess inventory and discuss a plan for converting it into cash.

Make sure you take possession of the items that you will be selling. You do not want to get into a situation where you find out after you have sold the item that the consignor has already sold it. You will also want to have the item on hand in case a potential bidder asks a question about it.

Setting Your Fee

There are about as many different fee schedules for consignment selling as there are consignment sellers.

You can find out what the going rates are in your area by visiting eBay's Trading Assistant Directory. There you can look up Trading Assistants (consignment sellers) in your area and view their fee schedules and policies.

However, to keep things simple I suggest the following fee schedule:

- Flat 40% commission on the final selling price of the item.
- You pay all Listing and Final Value Fees.
- Start each listing at $1.00.
- Charge exact shipping plus $2.00 per item for handling. (shipping and handling is not commissionable)
- Only accept items that will sell for or can be grouped into lots that will sell for at least $50.00.

This is the fee schedule that my friend uses to net over $25,000 a month from her eBay Auction Consignment business. It will save you a lot of headaches and makes it simple both for you and the retailer. It also leaves you free to negotiate a reduced fee for more valuable items if the retailer is hesitant.

"Make a Mint with a Highly Specialized Local Directory Project"

Here is a great money making idea sent in by one of my ezine subscribers, Skip Rosell. Skip is a real go-getter who is working on several business-to-business advertising sales projects.

Here is Skip's idea:

Use the classified section of your local paper online and find "Moving Sales" ads. These ads will have a street address and city but usually not a zip code. Copy the address and go to:

http://zip4.usps.com/zip4/welcome.jsp

Enter the address, city and state. This will give you the zip code of the house that is having the moving sale. Copy the complete address into a spreadsheet or database.

Do all the moving ads in your paper. You will find them under merchandise for sale, yard sales, etc. The best way is to insert the word "moving" into the search box of your local online paper's classified section.

Now that you have the names and addresses of the people moving sort them by zip code according to area. You know your area and if there are several zip codes within say 20 miles then you can group them together in one list.

Next, in the same newspaper search for "Cleaning". This will bring up all the ads that have cleaning in them. Most of these will be one-person businesses advertising cleaning services.

Copy these and bring back to a new spreadsheet or database. Almost all people that move will clean the place up and a lot of them would prefer to hire someone else to do it.

Now you are ready to make some money. How much money you make is up to you. It will be decided by how much "work" you do.

This is not hard work but you must start and work at it. You can do the same thing for all the painters, man with a truck, carpet cleaning, and many, many other businesses.

The best way to tell you how you make money with this business is to let Skip describe how it came about:

*I sold a cleaner an ad in my mini directory (**Editor's note: the mini directory is one of Skip's other Advertising businesses**) and then he asked if I knew of any other low cost ways of getting business.*

Since I was in the classified section of my local newspaper I told him he could send a post card to all the people that are moving. I explained how to do this and he asked how much I would charge to do it for him. I told him fifty cent each to address and mail a lead generating post card.

I then asked how many he would like mailed each week. Since he thought that these movers were about the best prospects he could get for his cleaning business, he said all I could get. I had to slow him down. I told him I can get about 15 per week in his zip code and I could work out from there and get as many as he wanted. The more he took the more travel he would have to reach each sale he made. We decided on 50 per week for a month's trial. Total $100.00 for a month.

I then printed up 15 sheets of 32lb stock with four post cards on each. Using an excel database I mail merged the addresses with a filter on the database for his zip code. Then did the same for the zip codes next to his until I reached 50.

Total time to print and address the cards was 15 minutes. It took me a little time to get the names into the database and doing only one business would not be very profitable. So I called a painter and told him about the post cards. Sold him on 50 post cards a week also.

Now why am I telling you about this business?

I have too much on my plate right now to start & test another unknown business. But it looks promising and I would like someone to try it out to see if it can be profitable. The price has to be tested, the wording on the post cards need testing, etc.

(end of Skip's message)

Skip has given you the basic concept so now I want to expand a little bit and show you how to make this more profitable.

First off, instead of sending a postcard for each business what will work better is to come up with a ***Moving Out Directory***.

People who are moving need the services of many different types of businesses and your directory would list these businesses. Contact each of these businesses as Skip explained above and sell them on the idea of being included in your directory. Here is a list of possible businesses that offer services to people who are moving:

- Gutter Cleaning
- Heating and Air Conditioning Servicing
- Pressure Washing
- Off Site Storage Facility (or PODs)
- Painting
- Moving Service

- Tree Removal
- Lawn Service/Landscaping
- Handyman
- Driveway Pavement Repair
- Deck Cleaning
- Window Repair
- Hauling
- Roofing Repair
- Property Management Service
- Exterminator
- Carpet Cleaning/Replacement
- Real Estate Agent
- Mortgage Broker
- Appraisal Service
- Home Inspection Service
- eBay Consignment Service *(don't you think people who are moving would love to make some extra cash for their unwanted items? Talk about a match made in heaven!)*

If you can get one business from each of these categories to pay you 50 cents per directory and you mail 200 directories a month that would earn you an easy $2000.00 a month. These businesses should jump at the chance to be in your directory because:

1. You offer them exclusivity (only one business per category allowed)

2. They could do this themselves BUT it would cost them more then 50 cents per address.

3. All the businesses above advertise in my local newspaper. They are spending much more then $100.00 a month and they are not getting anywhere near the targeted exposure you could offer them.

That is the idea in a nutshell. GO FOR IT!

"How To Uncover a Secret Stash of Valuable Treasure Hiding In Your Neighborhood"

My friend, Scott "Crash" Foster, stumbled onto a virtual gold mine in his area and he has allowed me to share the details in this report.

Here is what it is all about...

What Scott does is he looks on eBay for _hot items_ - items that are getting a lot of bids and selling for a consistently high price. Then he does a little research and determines if he can cheaply purchase these items in his area for resell on eBay.

One of the items that Scott has discovered is an extremely under-valued electronic product that he picks up in his area for pennies on the dollar and resells on eBay for a quick profit.

In fact, Scott routinely triples or quadruples his money on this product.

For example, just the other day Scott paid $25 for one of these hidden treasures and turned it around on eBay for $122.50. That's a 490% return -- _in three days!_

The really exciting thing is...

Scott's technique will work in any city or town in the US — no matter how large or small.

Because these little "hidden treasures" are everywhere just waiting for someone who *knows the secret* to pick them up for a song!

All you have to do is follow Scott's simple 4 step process:

- Run an ad in your local newspaper
- Wait for the calls (No selling at all!)
- Buy the item
- Sell it on eBay

Result: You can be banking the cash in as little as 3 days.

Sound unbelievable?

I decided to put Scott's technique to the test. Here are my results:

I used Scott's simply step-by-step system to purchase the item that he recommends. Using Scott's buying techniques I was able to purchase the item for $15.00.

On the same day I listed it on eBay. Scott told me the exact title to use for the auction as well as the item description.

I listed the item as a 3-day auction with a starting price of $1.00 (as per Scott's directions).

The item closed on Sunday evening at 9:00 EST. Here is an image of the closed auction:

Item	Start	End	Price	Title	High Bidder / Status	
	Jul-22-04	Jul-25-04 18:00:00 PDT	$112.50	*I Paid 15.00 for this item !*	goo	(11 ☆

As you can see the final price was $112.50. (for an item I purchased for $15.00.)

What you can't see from the above picture is that I had 13 bids for the item from 6 unique bidders. Bidding at the end was fast and furious because these items are Red Hot!

The person that won the bid PayPal'ed me the money the next day.

Here is a picture of the PayPal notification:

That represents a profit of $97.50 on my very first time trying this technique! Of course I had to pay the eBay listing fees and the PayPal fee but my total expenses were less then $10.00 giving me a Net Profit of $87.50.

So what exactly is this item that Scott has discovered?

Satellite TV Receivers!

For many people these receivers have out-lived their usefulness because they have cancelled their service.   So there are receivers just laying around in their garage or stored in a closet. That is why you can pick them up so cheap. But, by using eBay you can find other people who are frantically searching for this item. And they are willing to pay big bucks for it. New or used: they don't care. They just want them!

How many of these deals would you like to do?

Scott has written a detailed step-by-step course on exactly how to find and buy these receivers and exactly how to sell them on eBay.

In his complete course Scott shows you...

- Exactly what to buy.
- Where to place your *Items Wanted* ads. (for free!)
- Actual copies of Scott's *Items Wanted* ads that you can copy.
- How much to pay for the items.
- How to list the items on eBay for maximum profit.
- The exact description to put in the auction listing.
- The exact category to list the items on eBay.
- The best auction duration to use.
- A secret weapon Scott uses to create a bidding frenzy.

Hardly anyone knows about this secret little niche market and you can be one of the first to profit from it.

You can get the full details about Scott's course on his website at: www.ThisStuffSellsLikeCrazy.com

"How To Create Multiple Streams of Auto Pilot Income with Mini e-Books!"

Imagine making $1000.00 a day selling something you don't own to someone who you'll never meet and without the risk of going to jail! It's being done every single day by people all over the world working at home from their computers.

You may have heard of _Affiliate Marketing_ before but I have figured out a unique twist you may not have seen before.

For those unfamiliar with Affiliate Marketing is a brief overview...

In affiliate marketing, a company pays an affiliate (you) to generate sales from a button, banner, or link placed on your website, newsletter, email or pay per click ad.

There are thousands of companies in hundreds of industries that will pay commissions to you for leads, registrations or sales.

There are several large Affiliate Networks serving as go-betweens for companies and affiliates. For you as an affiliate, these Networks provide a valuable service: They collect payment from the merchant and consolidate affiliate reporting and payments.

An Affiliate Network brings together the companies and affiliates to form partnerships.

A partnership works like this:

The affiliate places links to the merchant's website from their own website, newsletter, emails, or Pay Per Click ads such as Google AdWords.

When a potential customer clicks through the link, they are sent to a specified page of the merchant's website. When they complete the action desired by the merchant, (fill out a form, buy something, etc.) the affiliate is compensated.

The Affiliate Network facilitates all aspects of the partnership and tracks all elements of the transaction.

Joining an Affiliate Network is totally free and there are no personal purchase requirements. You just fill out a form.

The top Affiliate Networks are:

<u>Commission Junction (CJ)</u>
<u>ClickBank</u>

Affiliate Programs are the ideal way to make money quickly and easily online. No need to come up with your own product or concern yourself with any of the hassles or headaches involved in actually stocking, selling or distributing a product.

Now, here is the *unique twist* for generating automatic affiliate profits that build from day one. This technique involves giving away – for free – special Mini e-Books.

A Mini-Ebook is a short market targeted report that can be created quickly for the sole purpose of providing concise, valuable information in order to pre-sell a particular affiliate product.

Imagine this – thousands of prospects download and read your Mini e-Book – and some of them buy the affiliate product you are promoting within the Mini e-book.

Let me show you an example of one of my mini e-Books. You can download it from:

http://www.business-ideas.biz/surveys

This free Mini e-Book is called; "*Can You Really Make Money Filling Out Online Surveys?*" It describes my experiences investigating and participating in online surveys. The important part is it has a link to a Survey Site I used to find the survey companies. That link is my affiliate link so anytime anybody clicks that link and orders I make 50% commission.

I created the Mini e-Book using Microsoft Word and then converted it to PDF format using a free utility called PDF995. You can download the PDF995 utility from http://www.pdf995.com/download.html. Once you download and install the software, you will see a new Printer Option called PDF995 when you print a document. Select this option and the software will create a PDF file from your document.

This Mini e-Book earns me money every month. Not a lot, mind you, but an extra $25.00 to $75.00 a month – sometimes more. The best part is after I created the Mini eBook and released it to the Internet, it became an automated money generator. People will download it day after day for years to come. Since my affiliate link is included in every downloaded copy, it will continue to make money for me perpetually.

Now imagine having 25 or 30 such Mini e-Books each one promoting a different affiliate program and earning you an extra $25 or $50 a month. You can see how that can add up fast can't you?

Extremely simple concept but very powerful.

Now, you are probably wondering what you do after you have created your Mini e-Book.

You need to promote it – i.e., let people know you have it and give them a way to download it.

One way to do this is to list your mini e-Book in **eBook Directories.**

An eBook Directory is a website that accepts ebook listings. These ebook directories are high traffic, so if you list your Mini e-Book people will visit and download it.

Here are several high traffic eBook Directories on which to list your Mini e-Book:

http://www.ebookdirectory.com/
http://www.free-ebooks.net/
http://www.jogena.com/ebookdir/ebookform.htm
http://www.wisdomebooks.com/add.html
http://www.mindlikewater.com/submitebook.html#Option%202
http://www.ebookpalace.com/cgi-bin/search/add_url.cgi
http://www.ebookjungle.com/submit.php
http://www.virtual-ebooks.com/addabook.htm

What kind of Mini e-Books can you create?

Anything that gives free, but quality, information about an affiliate product you can link to and earn a commission.

You can find affiliate products to promote by looking through the inventory at the CJ and ClickBank Affiliate Networks. Here are the links:

ClickBank Marketplace
Commission Junction Directory

If the prospect of earning extra money by creating quick and simply Mini e-Books interests you, you can find more information here: www.Mini-eBookProfits.com

"How To Position Yourself NOW To Cash In On the Next Big Internet Gold Rush"

There is a brand new money making opportunity developing on the internet as a write this article.   It's an opportunity that a few smart, tech savvy people have been secretly using for at least the past 7 years but for most internet users it is still a mystery.

I first hear about this opportunity just a few months ago. And truthfully, at first glace it sounded like some sort of stupid techie buzz word that geeks like to throw around to show people how smart they are.

That's where I was wrong.

You see, this opportunity is not really about a new technology at all. Rather, it is a faster, simpler and easier way for people to find the exact information they are looking for on the internet.

I'm talking about *Blogs.*

In the very near future Blogs will take over the internet and become as commonplace and widely used as search engines are today. And people that understand and start creating Blogs now will be the ones that cash in on the coming Gold Rush as the masses of internet users begin to use them on a regular basis.

What Exactly is a Blog?

Blog stands for Web Log. (weB LOG – get it?) It is basically a journal that other internet users can read on the web.

Generally, postings on a blog are arranged in chronological order with the most recent additions displayed first.

The activity of updating a blog is called "blogging" and someone who maintains a blog is known as a "blogger."

Blogs are usually tightly focused on a very specific topic. And that is what makes them so user friendly to internet users: Instead of searching through page after page of search engine listings looking for information on a specific topic, users can check a few blogs for the updated information about their desired topics.

Here are a few examples of blogs:

http://sweetestsuggies07.blogspot.com/
Blog about Sugar Gliders (a marsupial some people keep as pets)

http://www.profitwithgoogle.com/blogs/10/
Blog about Google Adwords.

http://thyroidhost.blogspot.com/
Blog about Thyroid Disease

http://gamesformoney.blogspot.com/
Blog about Gambling

http://vinodiversity.blogspot.com/
Blog about Australian Wines

http://www.textually.org/ringtonia/
Blog about Mobile Phone Ringtones

http://www.boxerdognews.blogspot.com/
Blog about Boxer Dogs.

And there are hundreds more at:

http://www.blogwise.com/

Tip: If you do a Google search for "blog" and "your topic" you can find blogs for just about any subject under the sun.

Ok, so now you know what a blog is – but how can you profit from them?

Let me demonstrate by showing you a particularly profitable blog and dissect what this blogger is doing to earn **$4583.33 a month.**

Go to http://www.mobiletracker.net/

This is a Blog about Mobile Phones. It is maintained by 19 year-old blogger Jon Gales and was featured in the October, 2004 issue of *Business 2.0.* MobileTracker is basically a compendium of news and reviews about cell phones.

Jon posts 4 or 5 items to the blog in the course of a day while relaxing on his parent's living room couch with his laptop.

One why Jon earns income is from the Google Adsense ads that are displayed right after each post. The ads look something like this:

When one of Jon's blog readers clicks on one of the ads Jon earns a small commission on the click. (Note: Google keeps the actual amount earned a secret but generally it is in the "cents" per click range.)

That doesn't sound like much but since Jon has over 200,000 unique visitors to his blog a month, these cents add up fast.

Jon also has other revenue sources on the site:

On the home page and news page there is a banner that leads to www.dataviz.com, a mobile phone company. You can bet that Jon is getting paid for displaying that banner.

In some of the posts there is an affiliate link to the product being discussed. For example, in a post about the new Audiovox 5600 smartphone, a message is included at the top of the post that reads:

> **Update:** *You can purchase the Audiovox SMT5600 at Amazon.com for -$25 after rebates. That's right, you get $25 back!*

That message is linked to Amazon.com via an affiliate url. So Jon earns money anytime someone purchases the product.

There are also links to other sites on the right hand side of every page. I can't be sure but those are probably paid links. (ie: the website pays Jon to include the link)

Ok, so that is how Jon is making money from his Mobile Tracker site. And according to the Business 2.0 article he is pulling in $55,000 a year working just 3 hours a day.

The point is, if a 19 year-old teenage blogger from Tampa, Florida can make $55,000 a year parked on his parents couch – *probably while watching TV* ☺ -- then you can too!

It took Jon a year and a half to build up the traffic to his site. So it does take some work. But, with the exploding popularity of Blogs you should be able to drive traffic to a blog faster then ever.

Anyone can earn money by using the exact technique that Jon has discovered:

- Pick a niche topic that is very popular.
- Set up a blog to contain your daily posts.
- Post four or five short news articles to your blog every day.
- Display Google Adsense ads on the articles and link to relevant affiliate products.
- Lather, rinse, repeat!

This is what you should do now...

1. Go to www.Blogger.com and set up a free Blog account. Follow the onscreen instructions and set up a sample Blog. At this point it doesn't matter what the topic is – just pick a topic you are interested in and start posting so you can learn the process.

2. Sign up for a free Google Adsense Account at: www.google.com/adsense/

3. Stay tuned to future updates of Kick Butt Business Ideas. I am going to be sharing with my subscribers the secrets I have uncovered about this exciting new opportunity.

So, if you are not signed up for Kick Butt Business Ideas (or if you want to sign up with your REAL email account instead of that crappy yahoo account that you never check) go here now and sign up now so you don't miss anything: http://www.kickbuttideas.com/12best/

I have an important update coming out in the next few days and you want to make sure you don't miss it.

"Behind the Scenes Secrets Of a Biz-Op Guru"

What I'm about to reveal to you here is a technique that is so secret you have likely never heard or read about it anywhere before.

I am going to tell you the REAL secret behind the full page ads you see in the business opportunity magazines. I am going to take away the smoke and mirrors, throw open the stage curtains and show you exactly how the high earning biz-op gurus REALLY make their money.

First, I have to give credit to Anthony Blake for some of the examples that I'm going to give you as I learned about them from a posting he made to a discussion forum. Anthony Blake runs his own discussion forum that is all about marketing products through the Internet and by direct mail. I would highly recommend you check out that forum, you'll learn a lot from the archives and get a lot out of participating. You will find it at www.ablake.com

How to Turn something that costs you little or nothing into your own personal cash machine.

So what is it that you can get for little or even no money and quickly turn it into a profit machine with just a little work?

There are a lot of sets of reports on the Internet that come with complete reprint/resale rights.

One of the most famous of these was a set of 650 reports that was originally published by Bill Myers on a CD ROM. When someone bought this CD, they also got the rights to reproduce and resell the reports as well as the rights to resell the resale rights!

Eventually several sites began to use them as a free gift or as a bonus item when you bought another product.

The bottom line is that with sets like this, no matter how you obtain your copy, you have the rights to use them as you wish.

BUT...

On their own these reports are totally useless. Sure there are still companies selling so called 'info-disks' and claiming that you can print off any one of hundreds of reports and sell it for $20 a time. That is nonsense – these reports have been sold and resold so many times that you can get them for free on the internet.

However, (and this is where you REALLY can profit)...

In a moment I'll tell you where to get hold of report sets like the one I mentioned. But first, let us look at a real life example of a product that was being sold for over $600.00 a copy and yet was built from freebies that came right off cheap info disks that the purchaser had full rights to use as he or she wished.

REAL LIFE EXAMPLE:

If you read biz-op mags then you'll have seen a full page ad with a picture of a couple on it (Russell Armstrong & Danielle Armstrong).

That ad is selling a book called "How to Make $15,000 A Month As Easy As Selling Lemonade From A Stand".

The book sells for $19.95, but there is an up-sell when you get the package that offers a much more expensive product.

The more expensive package is where it gets interesting, and is a very good study in the use of reprint rights.

In actual fact he offers two packages, one is what he calls his 'Basic package' which sells for a very un-basic $497, and the other he calls the 'Deluxe package' and costs $697.

The more expensive of the two is the most interesting to look at:

Here is what is contained in the deluxe package...

You get:

1) The Nuts & Bolts. The"Tell-All" Training Manual.

2) A Six-Tape Audiocassette Program

3) The Instant Business Package. This consists of a "Reprint Mail Order Manual" which sells a booklet called "The Secret to Mail Order Millions".

4) A Copyright License for "The Instant Business" Package which allows you to not only sell the info-product but to resell the rights to the package to others.

5) Camera-Ready Advertising for "The Instant Business Package".

6) An Advertising Directory.

7) Comprehensive Directory Of Book, Catalogue & Magazine Printing.

8) Internet Advertising Certificate.

9) Wholesale Supply Sources Directory.

10) Rights to the "How to Grow Rich in Mail Order" book.

11) Rights to "The Spare Time Mail Order Tycoon" book.

12) The "How to make $15k A Month Videotape Series".

13) The "How To Make $15k" Video Series Manual & Software Package.

14) 8 Coupons for "Via-Fax" Consulting.

Now that is a pretty fantastic sounding package isn't it? Imagine how impressive it looks when it's presented in a detailed piece of sales copy that expands each part of the package.

Remember, this is a REAL example. The above package is sold for $697 – so we're not talking pocket change product here!

Now what we're going to do is show you EXACTLY how he put it together. Prepare to be shocked! It was all put together from other people's material that he secured the reprint rights for. The incredible part is we are not talking about products where the re-print rights cost hundreds. The kind of thing he used was those 'info-disks' that you can get for 25 bucks.

Better still many of the report sets that this kind of product is created from are available either for free on the web or as bundles or bonus items for other products.

Now let's look at how this product was assembled:

1) The Nuts & Bolts, Tell-All Training Manual

This is a compiled manual of several of the reports available online for free or on those 600 special report CD ROM's. 12 Chapters culled from those special CD reports.

These so called, "Special Reports" have been circulating for years. Basically, you buy the reports or CD's for $39.00 - $99.00 and you get the right to resell them to others. Most of the time, you also have the right to resell the resell rights. And the people you sell them to also have the right to sell the reprint rights. And so on.

2) A Six-Tape Audiocassette Program

A lot of the content comes straight from the manual above (it's spoken by Russ Armstrong himself), there may be some original stuff added here and there.

3) "The Instant Business Package"

This is a reprint rights product that you can buy from small ads in the back of business opportunity magazines like Spare Time and Money Making Opportunities for $29.00 - $39.00.

4) A Copyright License for "The Instant Business" Package which allows you to not only sell the info-product but to resell the rights to the package to others.

5) Camera-Ready Advertising for "The Instant Business Package"

The above 3 items are actually all parts of the same package... you can get the reprint/resell rights to this from ads in various biz op publications.

6) The Advertising Directory is also just another report compiled from a set of free or cheap reports.

7) Comprehensive Directory of Book, Catalogue & Magazine Printing.

This is a book written and bought from John Kremer who wrote and publishes the book "1001 Ways to Market Your Books".

8) Internet Advertising Certificate

This is a certificate that entitles you to a free year's worth of classified advertising on Russ Von Hoelschers Internet site. Of course, you need to pay a $12.95 processing fee. (save your money. The advertising isn't even worth $12.95) Russ gives this away to attendees of his seminars and to those that buy his courses.

9) Wholesale Supply Sources Directory.

Yet another report compiled from the CD.

10) Rights to the "How To Grow Rich In Mail Order" book.

11) Rights to "The Spare Time Mail Order Tycoon" book.

The two above items are actually Reprint right items that can be gotten through ads in biz op magazines or from the web. The "How

To Grow Rich..." book was written by the Department of Commerce in the 1960's and the "Mail Order Tycoon" book was written by Stew Caverly and available through him.

12) The "How to make $15k A Month Videotape Series"

>From the title of the video series you'd think that they were created by Armstrong, but they're actually the 3 videos of Bill Myers presentation at Gary Hilbert's 1992 "Hurricane Andrews" seminar (it's Bill's "$30,000 A Month" video product). This is a set of videos for which resale rights are available at a fair price.

14) The "How To Make $15k" Video Series Manual & Software Package.

The manual is the handout from Bill's presentation at the Hilbert seminar. The software package is a set of spreadsheets that Bill created for his Business Toolbox CD, and a disk with the "593 Business Letters" product that Bill also created.

14) 4 pieces of paper with 2 certificates on each to use if you decide to fax Russ a question.

Now look at the above. Nothing original was created except for assembling the products together, repackaging them and selling them for a high price.

An excellent example of how to use reprint rights materials.

This must be working for Russ Armstrong as his full-size ads continue to run month after month (and advertising in these biz-op mags isn't cheap).

Now obviously he has purchased rights to some of these items and those rights are not always cheap (rights to a set of videos is usually $800). However you're not likely to shoot out and try to put together a package that sells for $697 on day one are you?

What you can do is get hold of report sets that have full reprint rights (and the rights to sell those rights) included in the purchase price.

Then take parts that you think are usable, update them, re-write them and re-format them into a new product.

Can you see the potential of working in this way?

Now the question is: Where do you find products that you can resell?

One source is Andy Brocklehurst's Inner Room. It contains a wealth of reports and products that you have full reprint rights to.

You could take some of these and re-work them into a new product. You could take some things as they are and put together a bundled package like the first one we discussed (it probably won't sell for $697, but you could easily create something that sold for $40, $50 or even $99 a copy).

You'll find the details about the Inner Room here: The Inner Room

Another way to find resell rights products is by doing a search on Google for "resell rights." For example, I just did a quick search and turned up hundreds and hundreds of listings for products with resell rights.

For video product resell rights do a Google Search for "resell rights" videos.   Here is an interesting one I found:

http://www.learn-futures.com/product/1-20a.htm

That is actually a DVD that you can get the rights to for $99.00. Put it together with a printed manual and maybe a couple of bonus reports and you have a product that you could sell over and over again for $200.00 -- $600.00.

Here is another site that has tons of resell rights products including the Bill Myers, "$30,000 A Month" product referred to above:

http://www.reprint-rights.com/product.htm

(note: the above are examples I pulled off Google – I have no financial interest in any of the products)

That's it! Take this basic idea and come up with your own product package that you can resell to others. You may become the next Biz-Op guru!